Masters of Music
THE WORLD'S GREATEST COMPOSERS

The Life and Times of

Irving Berlin

Mitchell Lane
PUBLISHERS

P.O. Box 196
Hockessin, Delaware 19707

Titles in the Series

The Life and Times of...

Johann Sebastian Bach

Ludwig van Beethoven

Irving Berlin

Hector Berlioz

Leonard Bernstein

Johannes Brahms

Frederic Chopin

Duke Ellington

Stephen Foster

George Gershwin

William Gilbert and Arthur Sullivan

George Frideric Handel

Franz Joseph Haydn

Scott Joplin

Franz Liszt

Felix Mendelssohn

Wolfgang Amadeus Mozart

Franz Peter Schubert

John Philip Sousa

Igor Stravinsky

Peter Ilyich Tchaikovsky

Giuseppe Verdi

Antonio Lucio Vivaldi

Richard Wagner

Visit us on the web: www.mitchelllane.com
Comments? email us: mitchelllane@mitchelllane.com

Masters of Music
THE WORLD'S GREATEST COMPOSERS

The Life and Times of
Irving Berlin

by Jim Whiting

Printing   2   3   4   5   6   7   8
        Library of Congress Cataloging-in-Publication Data
Whiting, Jim, 1943-
        The life and times of Irving Berlin/Jim Whiting.
             p. cm. — (Masters of Music: The world's greatest composers)
        Summary: A biography of the Russian immigrant who came to America as a boy and became one of the most successful composers of popular songs, including "White Christmas" and "God Bless America."
        Includes bibliographical references (p.) and index.
             ISBN 1-58415-215-X (lib bdg.)
        1. Berlin, Irving, 1888- —Juvenile literature. 2. Composers—United States—Biography—Juvenile literature. [1. Berlin, Irving, 1888-. 2. Composers. 3. Jews—Biography.] I. Title. II. Series.
ML3930.B446W45 2003
782.42164'092—dc21   2003000349

ABOUT THE AUTHOR: Jim Whiting has been a journalist, writer, editor, and photographer for more than 20 years. In addition to a lengthy stint as publisher of *Northwest Runner* magazine, Mr. Whiting has contributed articles to the *Seattle Times*, *Conde Nast Traveler*, *Newsday*, and *Saturday Evening Post*. He has edited more than 20 titles in the Mitchell Lane Real-Life Reader Biography series and Unlocking the Secrets of Science. He lives in Washington state with his wife and two teenage sons.

PUBLISHER'S NOTE: This story is based on the author's extensive research, which he believes to be accurate. Documentation of such research is contained on page 47.

        The internet sites referenced herein were active as of the publication date. Due to the fleeting nature of some Web sites, we cannot guarantee they will all be active when you are reading this book.

Contents

The Life and Times of
Irving Berlin

by Jim Whiting

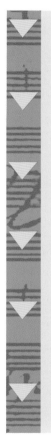

Irving Berling shortly after he was drafted into the U.S. Army during World War I at the age of 29. Though he never saw combat, he wrote a musical that raised money to help support the war effort.

The Song That United the United States

On the morning of September 11, 2001, millions of Americans awoke to horrifying news. Muslim terrorists had hijacked two jetliners and flown them into the two tallest buildings at New York's World Trade Center. A third hijacked airplane crashed into the Pentagon in Washington, D.C. Only the heroism of a group of passengers prevented a fourth from smashing into the White House.

As television viewers all over the country watched helplessly, billowing clouds of smoke and flames consumed the upper floors of the two towers. Some of the people who were trapped by the raging fires had to make a terrible choice: If they stayed where they were, they would be burned alive. Or they could jump to certain death. TV cameras showed some of these doomed people dropping to their deaths. Some fell together, holding hands in their last moments on earth. Others made final phone calls to their loved ones, then kicked out windows and jumped. These gruesome images were suddenly eclipsed by the sight of the two towers collapsing.

The death toll, which numbered in the thousands, included hundreds of New York City police officers and firefighters who had rushed into the buildings to try to save people. Only a few came back out.

The attacks created an unprecedented climate of fear and uncertainty in the United States. Suddenly U.S. citizens realized they were vulnerable to terrorist acts at home. But even though they were fearful, people tried to return to living as normally as they could. One thing that helped was attending sports events. It seemed appropriate that the New York Yankees played in the World Series that year. Everyone in sold-out Yankee Stadium and many millions watching on television had one memorable impression: During the seventh-inning stretch, a New York City policeman named Daniel Rodriguez stood near home plate and sang a song.

One of the towers of the World Trade Center begins to collapse shortly after being struck by a hijacked airliner on September 11, 2001.

New York City firefighters carry one of the victims of the World Trade Center attack away from the rubble.

That song was "God Bless America." Its words of patriotism and love of country provided comfort and support for millions of Americans.

"God Bless America" was composed by Irving Berlin. At the time of the attacks, Berlin wasn't fashionable or cool. The rise of rock and roll in the 1950s, followed by all the other pop music styles such as grunge, hip-hop, and heavy metal, had pushed his name into obscurity by the time of the attacks.

But in this time of stress and terror, people didn't want rock and roll. They didn't want hip-hop. They didn't want heavy metal.

What they wanted was music that made them proud to be Americans. What they wanted was music that emphasized what was good about their country. What they wanted was music that helped make them feel more secure.

They found all those things in "God Bless America."

Though probably only a few realized it, there was another reason "God Bless America" was so appropriate for that troubled time. The composer himself had had firsthand experience with a terrorist attack.

In 1893, when Berlin was a boy of about four or five, he and his family lived in a small village in Russia. One night a large group of their fellow Russians carrying torches poured into their settlement. They dragged some people out of their homes and beat them. They ransacked houses. They lit many houses on fire.

The victims hadn't done anything wrong, but they were Jewish. In Russia in the late nineteenth century, that was enough. What Berlin witnessed was just one more pogrom, one of hundreds of violent attacks on Jews that had begun in Russia a few years earlier.

Held tightly in his mother's arms, the little boy watched his familiar world dissolve in flames. The following morning the family looked at the charred ruins of their home. Almost all of their possessions were gone. Fortunately, no one in the family had been hurt—but maybe they wouldn't be as lucky the next time. The boy's father made a fateful decision. Even though they had lived in Russia for many generations, the family would leave everything behind and go to America.

This drawing shows a few of the millions of immigrants who arrived at Ellis Island during the latter years of the nineteenth century.

Russia's loss was America's gain. Four decades later, a famous composer named Jerome Kern would praise the man who wrote "God Bless America." Berlin's earliest boyhood memory of watching his house burn down made him grateful for the peace of his adopted country and the prosperity that it provided him.

"Irving Berlin has no 'place' in American music," Kern said. "Irving Berlin *is* American music." ◆

An announcement of a planning meeting, a flower and "God Bless America" inscribed on the ashy residue of a car window show that New York City residents remained positive in the aftermath of the September 11th attacks.

POGROMS

The violence that drove Irving Berlin and his family from their native Russia to the United States was hardly a unique occurrence. For many centuries Jewish settlements in Europe were attacked by the Christian majority. The Christians would justify their actions by saying that Jews were "Christ-killers," responsible for Jesus' crucifixion.

Eventually the Jews found a relative degree of security in Poland. But starting in 1772, Polish territory was carved up among several major European powers. By 1795 it had ceased to exist. Most of the Jews fell under Russian rule. By a decree of Czar Nicholas I in 1835, they were forced to live in what was known as the Pale of Settlement. This was an area that stretched from the Baltic Sea to the Black Sea. Many lived in cities and

Czar Alexander II

towns, while others had homes in small villages called shtetls. While occasionally they would be harassed, there weren't many large-scale acts of violence.

Czar Alexander II, Nicholas's successor, was assassinated in 1881. Almost immediately organized acts of violence against the Jewish population resumed. These were soon given the name of pogroms, a Russian word that means "riots" or "devastation."

Christians would pour into Jewish settlements, destroying property and attacking the inhabitants. While it wasn't uncommon for the rampaging mobs to kill Jews, the victims were more likely to be injured or made homeless. Most or all of their belongings would be destroyed. The Jews couldn't fight back. They were outnumbered to begin with, and if they tried to resist, the mobs would become even more violent.

There were hundreds of pogroms in the early to mid 1880s. Not unreasonably, Russia's Jewish inhabitants began looking for places to live where they might find safety. Many emigrated to the United States. Others settled as far away as Palestine and Australia.

Pogroms weren't the only reason to emigrate. Jewish boys as young as eight or nine could be drafted into the Russian army for periods of up to twenty-five years. To avoid this fate, some parents would deliberately maim their children. The most common injury was to chop off an index finger. That meant that the boys couldn't pull the trigger on a rifle, making them useless as soldiers.

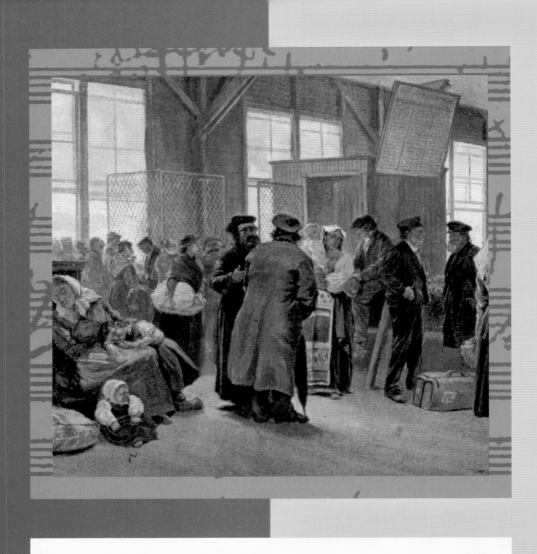

After their arrival at Ellis Island, immigrants had to pass through several inspection stations before they could be admitted to the United States.

Coming to the New World

Israel Isidore Beilin was the eighth and final child born to Moses and Leah Beilin. Moses Beilin was a cantor, or chief singer, in several Russian synagogues. While Israel's official birth date is listed as May 11, 1888, no one is sure if that is correct. Nor is anyone certain about his birthplace. Many people believe it was a town in western Siberia.

In fact, there are very few details about his life in Russia. His personal history began when his father made the decision to move to the United States after his family's close call in the pogrom. The two oldest Beilin children, already adults, chose to remain behind.

No one kept a record of the family's journey from the depths of Russia to New York City. It couldn't have been easy. The parents and their six children, ranging in age from nineteen to five-year-old Israel, had to cross hundreds of miles of rugged territory to Antwerp, Belgium. There they boarded a ship that would carry them across the ocean. They traveled steerage class, packed tightly below decks. Only rarely could they come up for fresh air. The rocking of the ship caused many to become seasick.

They arrived at Ellis Island in New York Harbor on September 13, 1893—just eight of the millions of immigrants who arrived each year. There the family name was changed from Beilin to Baline.

Soon they found a small tenement apartment in New York City's Lower East Side. It had four small rooms and only cold water. The children shared beds. The four girls used one, while Israel and his thirteen-year-old brother Benjamin slept in another.

The family had very little money. They had arrived at a bad time. The United States was in the midst of the panic of 1893, the worst economic depression the country had experienced since its founding. Many people were out of work. Moses Baline could find only part-time jobs, working as an inspector in a kosher slaughterhouse. His job was to ensure that meat was prepared according to strict religious rules. He made a little extra money by helping to conduct choir rehearsals.

The children had to help out financially. Israel—or Izzy, as he soon became known—and his six-year-old sister were the only ones who didn't have to work. The older children worked in what were called sweatshops, making clothing and other items for very little money. Working ten-hour days six days a week was common.

Despite the family's desperate condition, Berlin later told Michael Freedland in the biography *Irving Berlin,* "I never felt poverty because I'd never known anything else. We had an enormous family. Eight or nine in four rooms and in the summer some of us slept on the fire escape or on the roof. I was a boy with poor parents, but let's be realistic about it. I didn't starve. I wasn't cold or hungry. There was always bread and butter and hot tea."

There was also singing. Coming from a long line of cantors and other religious leaders, young Izzy had a fine soprano voice. He

sang at the local synagogue with his father. Music was all around him. It didn't cost anything to sing. Many poor families encouraged their youngsters to play a musical instrument. It could be their ticket out of poverty.

When he was seven, Israel began attending public schools. He did well for some teachers. But as Laurence Bergreen writes in *As Thousands Cheer,* one teacher complained, "He just dreams and sings to himself." One reason for his distraction may have been that he had landed in the United States without knowing any English. Eventually he would not only learn how to speak the language, but also how to use it very cleverly and with a great deal of originality. After school he made a few pennies a day to help out the family finances by selling a newspaper called the *Evening Journal.*

Many immigrants settled in communities where people all spoke the same or very similar languages. This drawing shows a Jewish section in New York City populated primarily by Poles and Russians.

Two years later, one of his sisters died at the age of twenty, probably of tuberculosis. And four years after that, in 1901, the family suffered an even greater blow: Moses Baline died.

Israel had no choice. He had to drop out of school to help support his family. Selling the *Evening Journal* became his full-time job. He sold the papers for a penny, but each copy probably cost him half that much.

The job almost cost him his life as well. One day he was down on the docks, selling papers and watching a ship being loaded. A crane hit him and knocked him into the East River. Someone finally realized that he was drowning and jumped in after him. When he was pulled out, more dead than alive, he was still clutching the few pennies for the papers he'd sold.

Izzy spent most of his time trying to help his family financially, but his life wasn't all work. In the summer he enjoyed going into the river by choice. He would take off his clothes, carefully hide them, then swim. But chances to have fun were few and far between.

His mother had established a custom. She would sit near the front door with her apron spread. When her children came home, each would throw the coins that he or she had earned that day into the apron. Almost every day, Izzy's contribution was the least.

At that age he was old enough to enter a sweatshop and begin making more money. But laboring in stifling warehouse conditions didn't appeal to him.

Eventually he came to a hard decision. He would leave home so that he wouldn't be a burden to his widowed mother and the rest of the family.

At thirteen years old, he was on his own. ◆

MOVIES

Almost from the time that photography was developed in the 1830s, people began to dream of adding motion to still pictures. Advances in film quality and experiments in high-speed photography helped pave the way for New Jersey inventor Thomas Edison and his assistant William Dickson. They produced a primitive movie camera called the kinetograph in 1892.

Thomas Edison

Edison believed that people would want to watch movies by themselves, so he and Dickson also invented a peephole viewer called the kinetoscope. The first movies only lasted about fifteen or twenty seconds. They were in black and white. There was no sound.

When kinetoscopes were opened to the public in 1893, they proved to be very popular. Dickson, the chief cameraman, kept busy producing new films to keep up with the demand. Soon other people invented movie projectors, which put the images up on a large screen. Now many people could watch a film together. Others invented cameras that were much smaller and more easily portable than the bulky kinetograph. That led to the production of longer films.

The first big hit was the *Great Train Robbery* in 1903. It was twelve minutes long and was one of the first films to tell a story. The most exciting part came at the end. One of the actors pointed a gun at the camera and fired it. People in the audience, believing that the actor was shooting at them, always ducked.

The late 1920s saw two of the industry's most important developments: the first "talkies," or movies with audible dialogue, in 1927, and the first Academy Awards in 1929.

Almost from the time of the first movies, inventors wanted to include sound. The first attempts failed because the pictures and the sound came from two different machines. The sound couldn't be synchronized with the actors' lips. Also, it was difficult to produce sound that was clear and loud enough for the large theaters that were being built as movies increased in popularity. Finally technological advances overcame the obstacles. *The Jazz Singer,* starring Al Jolson, was the first film with sound.

Movie technology has continued to make huge advances: Color film, improved sound quality, animation, and computer-generated special effects have helped the movie industry grow and prosper.

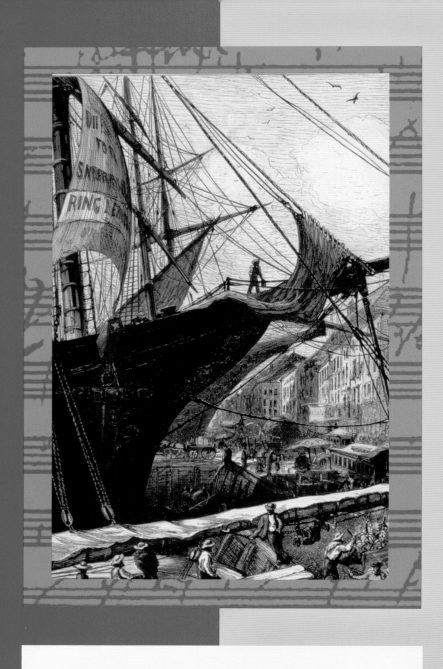

In the final decades of the nineteenth century, many sailing ships tied up at the docks in New York City. Loading and unloading them was dangerous work, and it wasn't uncommon for men to be injured or killed in accidents.

CHAPTER

3

First Successes

As Izzy wandered away from home, the thirteen-year-old had a definite plan. While he had been selling newspapers, sometimes he would enter saloons in the Bowery, an area of New York with many cheap theaters and places to drink. There Izzy saw something that amazed him. Children even younger than he was, called street buskers, would start singing. When they finished, the drinkers would toss coins at them. Sometimes the money would fall into the filthy sawdust that covered the floors, and the youngsters would eagerly dig for it. Izzy knew he was a much better singer than any of these kids, yet they were making more money than he was.

Izzy spent his first night away from home huddled under the stairway of a tenement house. The Bowery wasn't a place for the fainthearted. It was the only neighborhood in New York City without any churches. Murders were common. Izzy soon began singing in places with names such as Suicide Hall and The Bucket of Blood.

Izzy almost became a statistic himself. Early in his new career, he got into a fight with another boy. He was stabbed and was rushed to a hospital. He quickly recovered.

Once he started earning money, it wasn't hard to find a place to sleep. For ten cents he could get a cot in a nearby flophouse. Another nickel earned some privacy: a curtain around the cot. To prevent theft, the boy slept on top of his clothes. His shoes became his pillow.

On a good night of singing, he might earn fifty cents. If business was slow and he didn't make enough for a flophouse, there were always park benches.

But the boy knew that the busker's life was limited. Within a year he joined the chorus in a musical play. The play didn't do well and he lost that job. Undeterred, he headed uptown and auditioned on what was known as Tin Pan Alley. This section of the city was about a block long and had many music publishers. At that time, most of the money in music was in publishing sheet music. Tin Pan Alley churned out dozens of new songs every month.

These songs were very different from what had gone before. Earlier songs had been dignified and often contained a moral message. These new songs were rough-edged tunes that celebrated the new American strength. They were the first pop songs.

Many were performed in vaudeville acts. To help promote these songs, composers would hire "singing stooges." When a singer finished a new song, a stooge in the audience would immediately jump to his feet and sing the song again.

Izzy became a singing stooge. It wasn't dignified, but it was safer and paid more than being a street busker.

Then he got an even better-paying job at the Pelham Café in nearby Chinatown. He received seven dollars a week plus all the coins that were thrown at him. It wasn't an easy life. One night a customer shot and killed another while Izzy was singing. His hours

were also grueling: He worked from eight at night to six the following morning. This established a habit that he would retain for most of the rest of his life. He would work long into the night, then sleep in.

More important for his future career, he was allowed to use the piano in the back room before or after his shift. Izzy had an unusual method of playing: He only used the black keys. He soon learned how to pick out the tunes for popular songs. He also began writing parodies of many of them. It didn't take him long to become more and more popular with the regular customers.

The Bowery in New York City. It was one of the city's roughest areas, filled with cheap saloons and entertainment. Many homeless people lived there and the crime rate was high.

That was important because there was intense competition among the different restaurants. At one point the Pelham's owner, Mike Salter, was concerned because people were deserting his restaurant to hear a new song at a rival restaurant around the corner. He ordered Israel to write one that would bring those people back.

The result was "Marie from Sunny Italy." Written in 1907, it was the young man's first published work. Michael Nicholson composed the music, while Izzy wrote the lyrics. Izzy split the advance payment of seventy-five cents with Nicholson.

When it was published there was a typographical error on the cover: "Words by I. Berlin." Izzy liked the last name because it sounded more American than Beilin or Baline. By that time the young man had also decided that Izzy, his nickname, wasn't dignified enough, and Israel was too biblical and religious for popular music. He adopted the first name of Irving, after a famous British actor.

Soon afterward, the now-Berlin bought a used piano. Because he was still using just the black keys—which meant he only played in the key of F sharp—this piano had a special feature. It was a small wheel that allowed him to shift the keyboard. That way he could still play the black keys, but the melody would be transposed from F sharp into other keys. Later in his career the Steinway Company built a piano for him that replaced the wheel with a lever under the keyboard.

Because he didn't know how to read music, he would play or sing the melody for each new song when he was finished creating it. Someone else would write it down in musical notation so that it could be published. He continued this unusual method for his entire career.

All these real-life experiences gave the young man much better training than any school would have. Much later in life someone asked him how a more traditional musical education might have affected his talent. He replied that it would have ruined it.

Soon after "Marie from Sunny Italy" came out, Berlin and Salter parted company. The young man fell asleep in front of an open cash register. When his boss came in, the money was gone. Some people believe that Salter took it himself as a joke. Whatever actually happened, Irving was fired.

He quickly got another job, this time as a singing waiter at Jimmy Kelly's, a restaurant located closer to music publishers. He kept writing music in his spare time, and in 1909 he took another upward step.

He wrote "Dorando," about an Italian runner who nearly won the marathon in the 1908 Olympics but was disqualified when race officials helped him to cross the finish line. The song eventually earned $4,000 in royalties. A song later that year called "Sadie Salome" ended Berlin's days as a singing waiter and started his days working directly for a music publisher.

Soon afterward Berlin wrote a song called "My Wife's Gone to the Country, Hurrah! Hurrah!" It quickly became popular. A local newspaper asked him to provide new verses, and the wife of the publisher said she wanted to meet the composer. The paper was the *Evening Journal,* which he had sold for a penny a copy eight years earlier.

The success of that song also set him up for what would be his first real hit, "Alexander's Ragtime Band," which first appeared in 1911. Soon the song—and its young composer—became famous. Printers could barely keep up with the demand. "Alexander's Rag-

time Band" sold a million copies that year, and another million the following year as its popularity spread to Europe.

The song was even credited with saving dozens of lives. A fire broke out in a crowded movie theater and hundreds of patrons panicked. The pianist who provided musical accompaniment for the film quickly began playing "Alexander's Ragtime Band." Hearing the familiar music, the crowd calmed down. No one was even injured as everyone filed out in time.

For Berlin, that was just the beginning. The public scrambled to buy every new song that he wrote. He quickly became known as the Hit-Maker. The poor boy who had scooped pennies out of sawdust to earn a living was now making a six-figure income.

Berlin married Dorothy Goetz in February 1912. His life must have seemed a dizzying climb to the top.

But all too soon tragedy entered Irving Berlin's life. ◆

THE ROARING TWENTIES

One of the most colorful decades in American history was the 1920s, also known as the Roaring Twenties and the Jazz Age. The United States had become a major power because of its success in World War I, which ended with Germany's surrender late in 1918. Peace returned and prosperity soon came along with it.

Prohibition arrived the following year with the passage of the Eighteenth Amendment to the Constitution. The amendment prohibited the manufacture, transportation, and sale of alcoholic beverages. The intention was to improve people's home lives and reduce crime. But the opposite happened. Too many people still wanted to drink. Gangsters illegally imported alcohol and distributed it to equally illegal saloons called speakeasies. One of the most famous gangsters was Al Capone, who headed a vast criminal empire that made huge profits on the illegal sale of alcohol.

Al Capone

Meanwhile, with mass production pioneered by Henry Ford, automobiles became much more plentiful. That made it much easier for people to get around. Other popular technological advances included radios, record players, electric refrigerators, gas ranges, and even toasters.

The stock market took off. People made huge fortunes by buying stocks at one price and selling them at a higher price. Those prices just kept going up and up.

The symbols of the age were the flappers. These were boisterous, outgoing young women who wore clothing—especially short skirts—that would have been considered scandalous just a few years earlier.

All in all, it was an exciting time to be alive. But what goes up almost always has to come down. This was especially true of the stock market. Eventually the prices began to fall. No one wanted to buy. The prices fell even further, bottoming out in October 1929. Many people were ruined financially. Businesses closed. Millions of people lost their jobs. The stock market crash brought on the Great Depression.

With prosperity gone, Prohibition came under scrutiny. The controversial law was costly to enforce, and the alcoholic beverage industry, when legalized, could be profitable for the country. When Franklin Delano Roosevelt was elected president in 1932, one of his top priorities was to repeal the Eighteenth Amendment. He succeeded in doing that late in 1933.

Irving Berlin at work sometime during the 1920s, singing the words to a song he has just composed while accompanying himself on the piano.

CHAPTER
4

Making It Big

I rving Berlin's young wife, Dorothy, contracted typhoid fever during their honeymoon in Cuba. Five months after he had married her, Berlin buried her. Grief-stricken, the Hit-Maker went into hiding. Dorothy's brother urged him to put his sorrow into a song. The result: "When I Lost You." Lines such as "I lost the angel who gave me summer the whole winter through" described his anguish. Berlin later said that it was the only time he wrote a song specifically about his personal life.

In 1914 he composed the music for what became the prototype of Broadway musicals. *Watch Your Step* starred the famous dance team of Irene and Vernon Castle. Berlin would later maintain that opening night of *Watch Your Step* was the most thrilling of his life. It was the first time that he'd heard his music performed by a full orchestra. The musical was a huge success.

The decade that followed showed that Berlin had a great talent for business in addition to songwriting. He began composing the music to go with his words. That way he didn't have to split the money that the songs earned. Surprisingly, he still never learned musical notation. He always had someone else write down the actual notes. He built a theater called The Music Box so that he

wouldn't have to share the profits from his musicals. He supported the formation of the American Society of Composers, Authors and Publishers (ASCAP). ASCAP required licenses to perform works by its members, who therefore earned money every time their songs were played. He also formed his own music publishing firm, Irving Berlin, Inc., in 1914. He re-formed the company five years later under the same name. After a disagreement with his business manager in 1944, he established the Irving Berlin Music Company. It is still in existence today.

In February 1918, Berlin became a naturalized U.S. citizen. The country had entered World War I the preceding year and needed lots of men. Berlin, who was already twenty-nine and very famous, was drafted into the army. He wanted his valet to accompany him so that he wouldn't have to shine his own shoes or make his bed. Not surprisingly, his drill sergeant didn't like the idea.

For someone used to working all night and then sleeping late, hearing the bugler blow reveille at dawn was not pleasant. It inspired him to write "Oh! How I Hate to Get up in the Morning," which soon became popular among civilians as well as his fellow soldiers. He built on the success of the song to persuade the commanding general at his base to let him put on an all-soldier comedy revue to raise money. The base was located near the town of Yaphank, Long Island. Berlin called the revue *Yip! Yip! Yaphank*. Male soldiers had to play male and female parts, which added to the comedy. The show was a huge success. It was so funny that it even went on to Broadway. Because it was a comedy, Berlin removed one of the songs he had written for it. He thought "God Bless America" was too serious for a comedy.

In 1926, when he was thirty-seven, Berlin met Ellin Mackay, a twenty-two-year-old whose father, Clarence Mackay, was a million-

Irving Berlin performing in Yip! Yip! Yankhank, the musical that he wrote about life in the U.S. Army.

aire. Their house needed 134 servants to take care of its fifty rooms. Clarence Mackay couldn't stand Berlin. He disapproved of him for being Jewish, for being in show business, and for being an immigrant.

It didn't matter. The couple eloped. Although Ellin's father initially disowned her for it, the marriage turned out to be successful. The Berlins were married for fifty-two years and had three daughters.

Like many Americans—including his father-in-law—Berlin lost a great deal of money in the Great Depression, which began in

1929. But the loss provided one gain. Berlin and Clarence Mackay were reconciled.

Berlin wrote the music for a 1930 film, *Reaching for the Moon,* which featured a rising young singer named Bing Crosby. Studio executives, who often make sweeping changes to people's work, insisted on making the musical a straight comedy. It flopped.

Berlin kept working. In 1934 he was famous enough to be on the cover of *Time* magazine. The success of the movie *Top Hat* in 1936, starring the famous dancers Fred Astaire and Ginger Rogers, netted him $300,000. That was a huge sum of money for the time.

Irving Berlin with his second wife, the former Ellin Mackay. Ellin's father was very opposed to the marriage but eventually accepted it.

Berlin went to England in 1938 and saw firsthand that war was likely to break out again. He was asked to write a song to be sung on November 11 that year, the twentieth anniversary of the end of World War I. Unsatisfied with his first efforts, he remembered "God Bless America," the song that he hadn't used in *Yip! Yip! Yaphank*. He made a few changes and gave it to Kate Smith, "America's Songbird," who sang it on her national radio show. As soon as the show was over, the phones in Berlin's office started ringing. People all over the country wanted to buy a copy of the music.

Fred Astaire, shown in this picture, was born in 1899. He is considered by many people as the best professional dancer of all time. He made more than 30 movie musicals in which his dancing played a prominent role. Ten of those were with Ginger Rogers, his most famous partner. He died in 1987.

Berlin drew up a contract stipulating that all the profits should go to the Boy Scouts of America and Girl Scouts of America. According to the contract, "The completely nonsectarian work of the Boy Scouts and Girl Scouts is calculated to best promote unity of mind and patriotism, two sentiments that are inherent in the song itself."

It wasn't long before a movement began to make his song the national anthem, replacing "The Star-Spangled Banner." Though that never happened—Berlin himself opposed the idea—he did say, "Of all the songs I've written, this is the closest one to my heart."

"God Bless America" may have been the closest song to Berlin's heart, but for many people, another Berlin song holds that position.

On Monday morning, January 8, 1940, Berlin's employees were startled to see their boss come bustling into the office right after it opened. Because of his eccentric habit of staying up all night to compose and then sleeping all morning, it was unusual for him to come in this early.

That day, Berlin was a man on a mission. He hurried to his personal secretary, Helmy Kresa.

"I want you to take down a song I wrote over the weekend," Berlin said. "Not only is it the best song *I* ever wrote, it's the best song *anybody* ever wrote." ◆

BING CROSBY

Bing Crosby was the world's first great media superstar. In many ways, no one has ever surpassed him.

Harry Lillis Crosby was born on May 3, 1903, in Tacoma, Washington, the fourth of seven children. He enjoyed reading a popular comic strip known as *The Bingville Bugle.* The leading character, Bingo, had the same big ears that young Crosby did, so his friends began calling him Bingo. Shortened to Bing, it would be the nickname that would help make him immortal.

Crosby attended Gonzaga University in Spokane, Washington, intending to become a lawyer. Quickly realizing that he was more interested in music, he joined a local band, dropped out of school, and moved to Los Angeles. He got his first big break when the famous bandleader Paul Whiteman signed him on to sing. He was part of a trio called the Rhythm Boys, then he went solo. Within a few years he had become the most famous pop singer of his era, both live and recorded. He went on to have thirty-eight number-one hits, more than anyone else. The Beatles were next closest with twenty-four. And until recently, his recording of "White Christmas" was the top-selling song of all time.

He made his first feature film, *The Big Broadcast,* in 1932. More than sixty others would follow. For many years his name on a theater marquee guaranteed box office success. Many families still watch 1942s *Holiday Inn* during the Christmas season. It features Bing singing "White Christmas." In 1944 Crosby gleaned an Academy Award for his role as an Irish priest in *Going My Way.*

Crosby wasn't afraid to take unpopular stands. After he met the famous jazz musician Louis Armstrong, Crosby fought to give him a speaking part in one of his movies. At that time it was unheard of to give a black person such a role. In this and many other ways, Crosby tried to break down racial barriers in entertainment.

In his personal life, Bing Crosby married singer Dixie Lee, and the couple had four sons. Five years after she died in 1952, he married actress Kathryn Grant. They had two sons and a daughter.

By the late 1950s the rock-and-roll era had arrived. This new music wasn't anything like Crosby's relaxed, velvet-voiced style, and it was hard for him to compete. His popularity began to fade.

Crosby died a legend, on a golf course in Spain on October 14, 1977.

"White Christmas" was so successful that Berlin wrote an entire movie based on the song in 1954. It was the biggest box office hit that year and is frequently screened on television during the holiday season every year. Pictured are the movie's stars (left to right): Bing Crosby, Rosemary Clooney, Vera-Ellen, and Danny Kaye.

CHAPTER
5

"White Christmas"

The song that had Irving Berlin so excited was "White Christmas." As Philip Roth wrote in his novel *Operation Shylock,* "God gave Moses the Ten Commandments and then He gave Irving Berlin . . . 'White Christmas.'"

For many years it was the best-selling record of all time. Even today, more than sixty years after its composition, it remains among the top two or three. It may have even changed the way that we look at Christmas. Before the song was published, no one really cared whether there was snow on the ground on December 25. Today, as the date approaches, weather forecasters routinely make the likelihood of a white Christmas part of their reports.

The song may also have created an entirely new category of pop music. When Berlin wrote "White Christmas," there was almost no holiday music. That may have been why he decided to introduce it in the 1942 film *Holiday Inn.* Berlin insisted that Bing Crosby—the most popular performer of that era—star in the movie so that he could sing the song. To Berlin's surprise and disappointment, hardly anyone paid attention to "White Christmas" when the movie came out. Very few people bought Crosby's recording. Part of that was because Berlin didn't want to start advertising the song until the Christmas season.

Then something strange happened. Without any promotion, sales of "White Christmas" started to explode. Berlin was astonished. How could a song become a major hit without any publicity?

The answer was simple. As Jody Rosen explains in his book *White Christmas,* Berlin told his family at dinner one night, "The boys overseas are buying it."

World War II had been raging for nearly a year. Millions of young American fighting men soon would face bleak Christmases in damp, cold foxholes or storm-tossed ships. Many were still teenagers, away from home for the first time. "White Christmas" helped them remember bygone holidays with cheery fireplaces and brightly lit trees. They began asking for the music. And they got it.

Some of these fighting men were musicians. Before the war started, almost all radio programs were broadcast live, using studio bands and other musical groups. But now many of these performers were gone. To fill up airtime, most stations had to play recorded music. The overseas enthusiasm for the new song quickly reached the United States. It became common to hear "White Christmas" dozens of times every day.

The airplay started a stampede to buy either Crosby's recording of the song or the sheet music. By Christmas, the two versions had sold a combined total of over three million copies.

One reason for its popularity was that it became a symbol for why the country was involved in the war. *The Buffalo Courier-Express* wrote, "When Irving Berlin set 120 million people dreaming of a White Christmas, he provided a forcible reminder that we are fighting for the right to dream and memories to dream about."

Unlike nearly all other popular music, the song didn't fade after a few months. It continued to top the charts on succeeding Christmases and eventually became the most valuable copyright in music

Surrounded by soldiers during World War II, Irving Berlin plays some of his music. Berlin spent two and a half years during the war traveling around the world to perform for the troops.

history. Crosby's original master recording became so worn from making new disks that he had to rerecord the song. To this day, even though dozens of artists have sung "White Christmas," many people still associate the song with Crosby's version. It still makes Christmas a little more special for countless numbers of people.

In the 1940s Berlin became part of the war effort. Remembering the morale-building and money-raising success of *Yip! Yip! Yaphank,* he put together a similar musical for the new war. Called *This Is the Army,* it opened on Broadway in 1942. Soon the troupe headed for England to begin two and a half years of touring. A 1943 movie version allowed everyone at home to see it.

Not long after arriving in England, Berlin was invited to have lunch with the English prime minister, Winston Churchill. He expected that the conversation would revolve around show business. Berlin was startled when Churchill's first question was about war production in the United States. Although he didn't have any exact figures, he replied that everything was fine.

But Churchill kept asking Berlin political questions. The composer, feeling more and more uncomfortable, stopped answering them. Eventually Churchill ignored his guest and left the room. Apparently Churchill had confused Irving Berlin with a political commentator named Isaiah Berlin.

After leaving England, the cast sailed for Italy, where they faced German bombs and an eruption of Mount Vesuvius. After Italy came Egypt. Then Iran. Then a long journey to the island of New Guinea at the end of 1944.

Berlin—who traveled with the company and was one of the featured singers—never forgot that Christmas. In the steaming jungle, hundreds of GIs sang "White Christmas" for him. Even the natives translated it into their own language and sang it.

The war finally ended about nine months later. Berlin had been gone for several years with the cast of *This Is the Army*. He was eager to start composing again.

At first, Irving Berlin's music was as popular as ever. *Annie Get Your Gun* in 1946 was his most successful musical. Four years later, *Call Me Madam* also did very well. He used "White Christmas" again in a 1954 film called *White Christmas*. Crosby was one of the stars, and the movie was a huge box office hit.

Meanwhile a young singer in Memphis, Tennessee, was about to undermine Berlin's popularity. Elvis Presley's singing style would soon lead to a dramatic change in the pop music landscape. ◆

WINSTON
CHURCHILL

Many people consider Winston Churchill to be the greatest
statesman of the twentieth century. Born in 1874, he gradu-
ated from the Royal Military College at the age of twenty and
entered active duty in the British army. He fought in India and
the Sudan. At the same time he began what would become a
distinguished career as a writer. In 1899, during the Boer War,
he went to South Africa as a war correspondent. He was
captured but made a dramatic escape and almost overnight
became famous.

When he returned to England he entered politics. He won his
first election to Parliament in 1901. He quickly took on more
and more responsibility, and in 1911 was made first lord of the admiralty.
That meant that he was responsible for the Royal Navy, the largest in the
world. His leadership prepared England's navy for World War I.

The 1915 invasion of the Dardanelles in Turkey turned into an embarrass-
ing and costly military defeat. Churchill was forced to resign. It looked
like the end of his political career. To relax he took up painting and
became a very good artist. But his political skills were too valuable to be
wasted. He became involved in the government again just before the end
of World War I, serving in various offices until 1929.

For the next ten years he had little influence. With increasing alarm he
watched the rise of Hitler and the Nazi Party in Germany. He made
speeches warning of the danger that the Nazis posed. By the time
Churchill was appointed prime minister in May 1940, Germany was
winning the war. France surrendered soon afterward.

For nearly a year and a half, England stood alone. When the Japanese
attacked Pearl Harbor, Hawaii on December 7, 1941, the United States
entered the war. Though the fighting was bitter and millions of people
died, both Germany and Japan were defeated by 1945.

The English people believed that a new government could run the
country better in peacetime. They voted Churchill's Conservative Party
out of office.

The Conservatives returned to power in 1951. Churchill, by then seventy-
seven, once again became prime minister. Many honors began coming
his way. He received the Nobel Prize in literature in 1953. The Royal
Academy had a showing of his paintings in 1958. When he died in
January 1965 at the age of ninety, his funeral was one of the largest ever
held in England.

Elvis Presley as a young man. He became famous in 1956 for his first big hit, "Heartbreak Hotel," and quickly followed with other songs such as "Jailhouse Rock," "Hound Dog," "Blue Suede Shoes," "Love Me Tender" and "Are You Lonesome Tonight." He starred in more than 30 movies and many television specials in addition to hundreds of live concert appearances. Known as "The King," he is one of the very people who is instantly recognizable with just his first name.

CHAPTER 6

Out of Fashion

I n 1956, twenty-one-year-old Elvis Presley roared onto the pop music scene with his first big hit, "Heartbreak Hotel." Rock and roll was suddenly the rage. It was completely different from Berlin's music.

The following year Presley included his version of "White Christmas" in *Elvis' Christmas Album.* A jealous Berlin called radio stations all across the country. He asked them not to play anything from the album.

Hardly anyone honored his request. The man who had shaped the country's taste in popular music for more than four decades had lost his influence. A new "king"—which soon became Presley's nickname—had emerged to rule America's music culture.

In 1962 Berlin wrote what would be his final musical. Called *Mr. President,* it was about the new couple in the White House. Despite the huge personal popularity of Jackie and John F. Kennedy, the musical was a flop. *Time* magazine harshly called it the "worst musical on Broadway."

Two years later an English singing group called the Beatles came to the United States. The transformation of pop music was complete. Few people were interested in Irving Berlin anymore. "White

Christmas" was always popular during the holiday season, but as the years went by fewer and fewer people associated the song with its composer.

Berlin realized that his time was up. "It was as if I owned a store and people no longer wanted to buy what I had to sell," he admitted in the introduction to Robert Kimball and Linda Emmet's book *The Complete Lyrics of Irving Berlin.* "It was time to close up shop."

He continued to write songs, but they were mostly for an audience of two: himself and his wife. They became very reclusive, rarely leaving their New York City apartment.

"I'm sure he regarded himself as the greatest American songwriter, but insecurity tormented him all his life," said Lawrence Bergreen, author of *As Thousands Cheer: The Life of Irving Berlin.* "But at the same time he was as astonished as anyone that he was so successful. Underneath it all he was just Izzy Baline from the Lower East Side who was utterly dependent on his audience to keep him happy."

Berlin was also capable of generosity. In 1979, a documentary film called *Best Boy* was nominated for an Academy Award. It included a scene in which a mother placed her son, a mentally retarded man, in an institution. She cried as she left him behind, and began singing one of Berlin's songs. It was one of the movie's most powerful moments.

But there was a problem. Because the mother's action had been spontaneous, the filmmaker, Ira Wohl, hadn't applied to Berlin's music company for permission to use the song. The film was released before he had asked the company for a license.

Berlin's lawyers turned them down. That meant that the film couldn't be considered for the Academy Award. Desperately, Wohl asked a friend of Berlin's to phone the composer. The tactic was

successful. Berlin called back and said, "They will get the license." *Best Boy* went on to win the Academy Award.

Berlin's final public appearance had been six years earlier at a White House reception honoring returned prisoners from the Vietnam War. He led the gala audience as they sang "God Bless America." In 1988, a tribute at New York's Carnegie Hall honored his 100th birthday. Many of the country's most famous musicians took part, including Frank Sinatra, Natalie Cole, Willie Nelson, Leonard Bernstein, and Isaac Stern. It soon became an Emmy award-winning television special.

By then Berlin had received many other honors. "White Christmas" won an Oscar in 1942 for best song. Berlin was awarded the army's Medal of Merit, a Congressional Gold Medal for "God Bless America" and other patriotic songs, and the Freedom Medal from President Gerald Ford. A postage stamp with his photo and the manuscript of "God Bless America" would be issued in 2002.

When he died in his sleep on September 22, 1989, a few of his faithful fans met in the street outside the New York City apartment where he had lived for many years. They sang "God Bless America" in his memory.

Almost exactly twelve years later, police officer Daniel Rodriguez and millions of other Americans would sing the same song.

The final words, "My home sweet home," are especially fitting for his life. The boy who fled from Russia because of persecution had indeed found a "home sweet home" in the United States. He was always grateful to his adopted country. He repaid that gratitude by giving it 1,000 songs (35 of which were number-one hits, more than any other composer), 30 Broadway shows, and 17 Hollywood musicals. ◆

Selected Works

Songs

"White Christmas"
"God Bless America"
"Alexander's Ragtime Band"
"Blue Skies"
"There's No Business Like Show Business"
"Cheek to Cheek"
"Let's Face the Music and Dance"
"Puttin' on the Ritz"
"A Pretty Girl Is Like a Melody"

Movies

Top Hat
Holiday Inn
White Christmas
Follow the Fleet

Musicals

Yip! Yip! Yaphank
Watch Your Step
Annie Get Your Gun
Call Me Madam
Face the Music
Louisiana Purchase
This Is the Army

Chronology

1888 Israel Isidore Beilin is born on or about May 11 in Russia
1893 Arrives in New York City
1895 Begins attending public school
1901 Father dies; Israel leaves home to become street busker
1904 Becomes singing waiter at Pelham Café
1907 "Marie from Sunny Italy" is first published song
1909 Publishes "Dorando," "Sadie Salome," and "My Wife's Gone to the Country, Hurrah! Hurrah!"
1911 "Alexander's Ragtime Band" becomes first major hit song
1912 Marries Dorothy Goetz, but she dies within five months
1914 *Watch Your Step,* first full-length musical, opens; forms Irving Berlin, Inc., his own music publishing company, which becomes today's Irving Berlin Music Company
1918 Becomes naturalized U.S. citizen; is drafted; produces *Yip! Yip! Yaphank,* a musical comedy about life in the army
1920 Builds The Music Box Theatre
1926 Marries Ellin Mackay
1927 His "Blue Skies" is the first song heard on a "talkie," a movie with sound
1934 Appears on cover of *Time* magazine
1938 "God Bless America" is performed for the first time
1940 Composes "White Christmas"
1942 Writes *This Is the Army*
1946 *Annie Get Your Gun* becomes his most successful stage work
1954 Uses "White Christmas" again in movie *White Christmas*
1962 *Mr. President* is final stage work
1973 Makes final public appearance
1988 Receives 100th birthday tribute
1989 Dies of natural causes on September 22

Timeline in History

1888 George Eastman invents the first handheld camera.
1893 Henry Ford builds first automobile.
1896 Electric stove is invented; first modern Olympic Games held in Athens, Greece.
1903 Wright brothers make first airplane flight.
1917 United States enters World War I.
1918 World War I ends.
1920 In Pittsburgh, KDKA is the first radio station to be licensed.
1927 *The Jazz Singer* is the first movie to have spoken dialogue.
1929 Stock market crash brings on the Great Depression in United States.
1932 Franklin D. Roosevelt wins U.S. presidential election in landslide victory.
1941 United States enters World War II.
1945 World War II ends.
1948 Long-playing records (LPs) introduced.
1950 Korean War begins, ending in 1953 with a truce.
1956 Elvis Presley's "Heartbreak Hotel" begins a music revolution.
1964 British singing group the Beatles appear on Ed Sullivan TV show and set off wave of "Beatlemania" in the United States.
2002 U.S. Postal Service issues Irving Berlin stamp.

Further Reading

Works Consulted

Antin, Mary. *Promised Land*. New York: Modern Library, 2001.
Bergreen, Laurence. *As Thousands Cheer: The Life of Irving Berlin*. New York: Viking Penguin, 1990.
Freedland, Michael. *Irving Berlin*. New York: Stein and Day, 1974.
Furia, Philip. *Irving Berlin: A Life in Song*. New York: Schirmer Books, 1998.
Hamm, Charles. *Irving Berlin. Songs from the Melting Pot: The Formative Years, 1907–1914*. New York: Oxford University Press, 1997.
Jablonski, Edward. *Irving Berlin: American Troubadour*. New York: Henry Holt and Company, 1999.
Kimball, Robert, and Linda Emmet. *The Complete Lyrics of Irving Berlin*. New York: Knopf, 2001.
Rosen, Jody. *White Christmas: The Story of an American Song*. New York: Scribner, 2002.

Web Addresses

"Irving Berlin on Film" http://www.brightlightsfilm.com/30/irvingberlin1.html
http://www.archives.gov/publications/prologue/summer_1996_irving_berlin_1.html
http://www.kcmetro.cc.mo.us/pennvalley/biology/lewis/crosby/Berlin2.htm

Index